THE WEEKEND DECORATOR
FURNITURE

THE WEEKEND DECORATOR

FURNITURE

PAMELA INNES
WORKPAPER DESIGNS BY SARA JOHN

AURUM PRESS

For my mother, Jo

ACKNOWLEDGEMENTS

The author and publishers would like to thank the following for their help in the creation of this book: Keith Warwick, Robert Lillis, Sheila Wilson, Huntley Hedworth and Cotham Hardware in Bristol; Fiona Allerdyce-Lewis in Dumfries; and Sue Fox in Somerset.

A NOTE ON QUANTITIES
Paint quantities are given in millilitres, litres and grammes (for powder paints). Approximate conversion to U.S. measurements are as follows:

100 ml = $3^{1/2}$ fluid ounces
1 litre = $1^{3/4}$ pints
5 litres = 1 gallon
100 grams = 4 ounces

First published 1996 by Aurum Press Limited, 25 Bedford Avenue, London WC1B 3AT

A catalogue record of this book is available from the British Library.

ISBN 1 85410 427 6

Photography by Marie-Louise Avery and Jonathan Metcalf
Styling by Margaret Caselton
Edited by Judy Spours
Designed by Donald Macpherson

Printed in Singapore by Imago

CONTENTS

INTRODUCTION

I first became aware of painted furniture as a rebellious twelve-year-old, when my enlightened god-mother trailed me round the London museums and galleries on what was supposed to be a consciousness-raising introduction to 'Culture'. I hated every minute of it. The National Gallery proved a disaster – Rembrandt and the Impressionists failed to inspire – and I sat engrossed in an old copy of The Beano throughout a weighty lecture on Ancient Egypt at the British Museum.

After two days, my well-meaning godmother was about to throw in the towel, and hurl me onto the first fast train home, when the moment of enlightenment struck – in the Victoria & Albert Museum. There I suddenly came across what I considered to be true genius. I saw furniture from all over the world and from all centuries which people had painted, carved and decorated with great skill and imagination – just to use at home. I cannot honestly say that my excitement in gazing upon these colourful pieces, so lovingly embellished throughout history, was quite what my godmother had hoped for, but they did inspire in my small, barbaric breast a love of colour and design which has remained ever since.

Throughout history we have been adapting and experimenting with the places we live in and call home. More than anything else, it is the way in which we have organised, decorated and furnished our houses which most reflects the significant changes in social and domestic life.

Five hundred years ago, furniture for an affluent household consisted of four basic items – table, chairs, chests for storage and, most valued of all, the bed. A good, big bed was handed down from generation to generation and conveyed considerable status in the fifteenth century. Later, as people began to accumulate more household goods, a chest with drawers was added to the list, and as a wider section of society became more literate, a desk for writing and shelves for books became essential. Perhaps surprisingly, the necessity for these basic pieces has not changed much over the following centuries.

Inevitably, some forms of furniture have been subject to the whims of fashion. In the twentieth century, large wardrobes and bathroom furniture have evolved into 'built-in' pieces to fit into smaller houses. The food cupboard has given way to the refrigerator and the Victorian dresser has come and gone and come again as a fashion item. Other pieces are now completely redundant. The days of the status-symbol wireless set or cocktail cabinet have waned, giving way to home computers, videos and microwave ovens. Even the large television console seems to have had but a limited life.

Whilst it is easy to understand our preference for comfort, from the simple bench to today's upholstered sofas, it is much harder to explain the human need, from time immemorial, to decorate functional domestic furniture. There has always existed an innate desire, even within the earliest semi-skilled joiner working rough with crude tools, to add something of himself to the basic tables and chairs he was making, and to take time to carve, say, rondels and decorative borders into the wood. Mass-production, with its endless repetition of the same form, is unable to provide the spirit, the sense of well-being and joy which those earlier, decorated pieces inspired.

I have been travelling around Britain teaching paint techniques for the past five years, and it has become obvious to me that what most excites students is the chance to restore a neglected, sometimes ugly, piece of furniture, and to turn it into something usable and unique. Wonderful ideas have come from people who would never dream of putting a brush to canvas but who, when given a gentle nudge in the right direction, reveal an eye for colour and a long-forgotten talent for decoration. I hope that this book will encourage you to take that step. Nowadays most of us have to live with mass-produced furniture because it is affordable and accessible, but the effect it produces is often one of boring uniformity. We all should have at least one exciting piece of furniture at home.

Have you looked in your attic recently? Is there a neglected piece of furniture lurking there – a battered

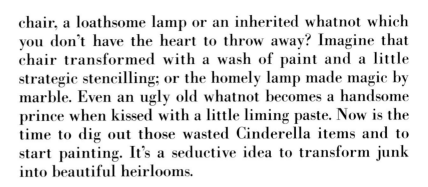

chair, a loathsome lamp or an inherited whatnot which you don't have the heart to throw away? Imagine that chair transformed with a wash of paint and a little strategic stencilling; or the homely lamp made magic by marble. Even an ugly old whatnot becomes a handsome prince when kissed with a little liming paste. Now is the time to dig out those wasted Cinderella items and to start painting. It's a seductive idea to transform junk into beautiful heirlooms.

To create the projects in the book and to prove what can be achieved, we raided junk shops and DIY stores in search of the blandest, cheapest pieces of furniture we could find. The techniques demonstrated are those which have been used on decorative furniture by painters and craftsmen for centuries, and I have added a little modern technology and some professional tips to help you to achieve perfect results. None of the techniques we use is difficult – as long as you are prepared to spend a little time. At the back of the book are workpapers, which can be detached for your own use, featuring the design motifs used in the projects. Alongside our main projects, we have also used the same design ideas on more modest pieces of furniture and decorative items. These may be a good way for you to try out the new skills demonstrated in the book, and most of them were completed within a few hours. At the back of the book there is also a section outlining basic techniques for the preparation of furniture which is to be decorated.

Weekend furniture painting is therapeutic. Apart from the initial satisfaction of the transformation, there is the lasting pleasure of living with the piece afterwards. After all, when you enter a home it is the personal touch of colour and creativity – just as much as the aroma of a good meal cooking – which cheers the heart and brings a feeling of warmth and well-being.

SILK UPHOLSTERED CHAIRS

In a secondhand shop full of junk furniture, we found these turn-of-the-century chairs huddled together like a gang of troublemakers. They were large, solid and somewhat menacing. Rancid horsehair pushed through their grimy upholstery like knees through ripped jeans. Padded shoulders were so thick with ancient dust that they resembled scuffed black leather. These were seats which could never be improved, delinquent chairs which would resist any attempt to reform them.

Sara, who likes a challenge, wanted to buy them immediately. Preferring the odds to be stacked a little more in my favour, I turned my back on them. I was drawn to a quieter-looking set. But the gang crowded around me and, rather weakly, I sat on one of them. It was surprisingly comfortable: these days they don't stuff chairs the way they used to. Finally, we bought them very cheaply as a job lot. They jostled about in the back of the car on the way home. I felt threatened.

Taking off the original, woolly upholstery was like a journey to hell and back. The chairs had been well made, and these boys were not about to give up their rags without a struggle. A good wash outside with a heavy-duty hosepipe revealed surprising treasure in the form of some very attractive carving on the upper parts of the chair backs.

Once clean and stripped, our delinquents looked disarmingly vulnerable, but I decided to get my own back on them anyway and dress them in hand-painted silk when I knew that they were yearning for leather. However, to retain a little of their street credibility and in sympathy with their battered personalities, we 'aged' the new paint applied to the frames. Ageing, or antiquing, is an easy technique, especially suited to older furniture which needs a soft, understated appearance. In its simplest form, a coat of new paint is brushed over bare wood and then rubbed back with sandpaper or wire-wool until the wood underneath shows through the paint. The whole piece is then washed over with a 'dirtied' varnish to simulate the dust of ages.

With thoughts of their original Edwardian splendour in mind, we painted the frames a rich, creamy white to match the silk chosen for the upholstery. Then we rubbed them over with diluted emulsion paint and methylated spirits to bring the carving on the chair backs into soft relief. I must admit that by now, unbelievably, the chairs were beginning to look... rather noble.

SILK UPHOLSTERED CHAIRS
Techniques used:
Antiquing and Silk painting

SHOPPING LIST

Chair Frames (Antiquing)

A set of inexpensive upholstered dining chairs
Medium grade sandpaper
Fine grade wire-wool
2   1½-inch decorating brushes
Half-litre wood primer
Litre cream emulsion paint
Burnt umber acrylic tube colour
Methylated spirits
Half-litre matt polyurethane varnish
Soft, lint-free cloths
No. 4 watercolour brush

Chair Upholstery (Silk Painting)

Workpaper Design A
Dressmaker's transfer paper
HB pencil
Medium or heavy weight upholstery silk cut to correct
dimensions
125 ml pots of silk paints in blue, brown, yellow and dusky
pink
125 ml pot of colourless silk wax resistor
Stretcher frame or old picture frame
No. 4 and No. 2 watercolour brushes

ANTIQUING THE FRAMES
Step-by-step

1.

If the chairs are thickly covered in dark stain or old paint, they should be stripped back to the bare wood (see page 77). Otherwise, sandpaper thoroughly, using wire-wool around the edges and mouldings. Paint the chairs with a thin coat of wood primer. Allow to dry.

2.

Paint the frames with a smooth coat of cream emulsion. Allow to dry and sand lightly. Cover with a second coat of cream emulsion and allow to dry. Sand lightly and wipe over with a soft, damp cloth.

3.

Mix the antiquing glaze by combining ¹/₂-inch squeeze of burnt umber acrylic paint with a little water and two tablespoons of the cream emulsion. Transfer the mixture to a container and add 250 ml cream emulsion and 50 ml water. Mix thoroughly.

4.

Paint the glaze solution over all areas of the chair frame, working it well into any mouldings and carvings. Allow to dry.

Applying the first coat of cream emulsion.

Working antiquing glaze into the mouldings.

ANTIQUING THE FRAMES
Step-by-step

5.

Dip a soft, lint-free cloth (which will not deposit fibres) into methylated spirits and rub the chair frame all over, removing parts of the glaze where the chair would naturally wear - around edges and carvings. The result should be a glazed frame with areas of cream paint revealed.

6.

Highlight any raised carving or moulding with the No. 4 watercolour brush and un-diluted cream emulsion.

7.

When thoroughly dry, varnish the entire frame with matt polyurethane varnish, applying a second coat for lasting protection.

Using a soft cloth with methylated spirits to remove the glaze in certain areas.

Highlighting the mouldings with cream emulsion.

PAINTING THE SILK UPHOLSTERY
Step-by-step

1.

Transfer Workpaper Design A onto your chosen fabric (see page 80). The workpaper size can be reduced or enlarged on a photocopier to fit a different size of chair.

2.

Stretch the transferred fabric across a stretcher or old picture frame and pin it into position.

3.

Draw over the pencilled design with wax silk-resistor, holding the bottle vertically with tip pressed firmly on the fabric. The resistor must penetrate the fabric to prevent the silk paints from flowing beyond the lines of the design. Allow approximately one hour to dry.

4.

Using a No. 4 watercolour brush, begin to colour inside the design with silk paints. Start with the application of dusky pink in the centre of the area to be covered. Encourage the colour to flow towards the waxed outlines of the design by pushing it with a wet brush, adding more colour and water if necessary.

Transferring the workpaper design onto the silk upholstery material.

Drawing round the design with wax silk-resistor to prevent the silk paints running.

PAINTING THE SILK UPHOLSTERY
Step-by-step

5.

Use the dusky pink to shade around the edges of the design, and yellow and brown to provide high- and low-lighted areas. With a clean No. 2 watercolour brush, paint in circled areas of the design in blue.

6.

Allow the silk paints to dry for forty-eight hours and then heat-set them by passing over with a cool iron. The design can now be safely dry-cleaned or washed.

Completing shading and highlighting on the inside of the design motifs.

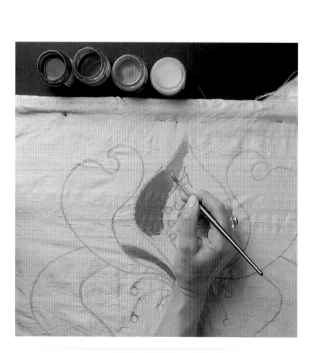

Starting with dusky pink and yellow in the centre of the design.

Painting in the circles in the design with blue.

PAINTING THE DESIGN ONTO CHAIRS WITH WOODEN SEATS AND BACKS

1.

If the chairs are covered in a dark stain or old paint they should be stripped back to the bare wood (see page 77). Otherwise, sandpaper thoroughly, using wire-wool around the edges and mouldings. Paint the entire chair with a thin coat of wood primer and allow to dry thoroughly.

2.

Follow the instructions given for antiquing the chair frames on pages 13-14, but apply the antiquing technique over the entire chair – frame, seat and back. Allow to dry and leave unvarnished for the time being.

3.

If necessary, reduce or enlarge Workpaper Design A to fit your chosen chair seat and back. Attach the workpaper using masking tape, and transfer using a hard pencil (see page 80), taking care not to press too hard and score the wood. Check that the whole design has been transferred and clean up any smudges and stray pencil lines with a soft eraser.

4.

The colours we used for our chairs were dusky pink, brown, yellow and blue. Test pots in vinyl matt emulsion will provide enough paint to decorate eight chairs, or if you prefer, acrylic (water-based) tube colour mixed to single-cream consistency with water can be used.

5.

Using a No. 6 watercolour brush and the pink colour, paint in the large leaf areas of the design. If the paint you are using looks a little bright and new, tone it down by mixing with a small amount of brown to produce a softer shade of dusky pink.

6.

While the paint is still damp, shade in the edges and tips of these larger leaves with the yellow paint, blending and shading the pink and the yellow paints together where they meet. Allow to dry.

7.

Using a No. 2 watercolour brush, paint in the stems and finer details with dusky pink and allow to dry.

8.

Paint in the circled areas (seeds and stamen ends) using the No. 2 watercolour brush and blue paint.

9.

When dry, paint with two smooth coats of varnish, sanding each coat when dry. The chairs can now be sponged clean when necessary.

MAKING CHAIR CUSHIONS

Workpaper Design A can easily be adapted using the method described on pages 15-16 when making loose, squab cushions to fit and tie onto plain wooden chair seats. Simply cut the fabric to size, allowing three-quarters of an inch all round for the seams, and transfer and paint the design onto the fabric as described. Toning braid or ribbon can be used as tie-ons for attaching the cushions to the chairs.

PAINTED SILK LAMPSHADES

Here the same silk painting technique has been used to decorate a
pair of plain silk lampshades. A simple motif has been painted in
one colour only to create tablelamps in colours darker than, but
toning with, the upholstered chairs.

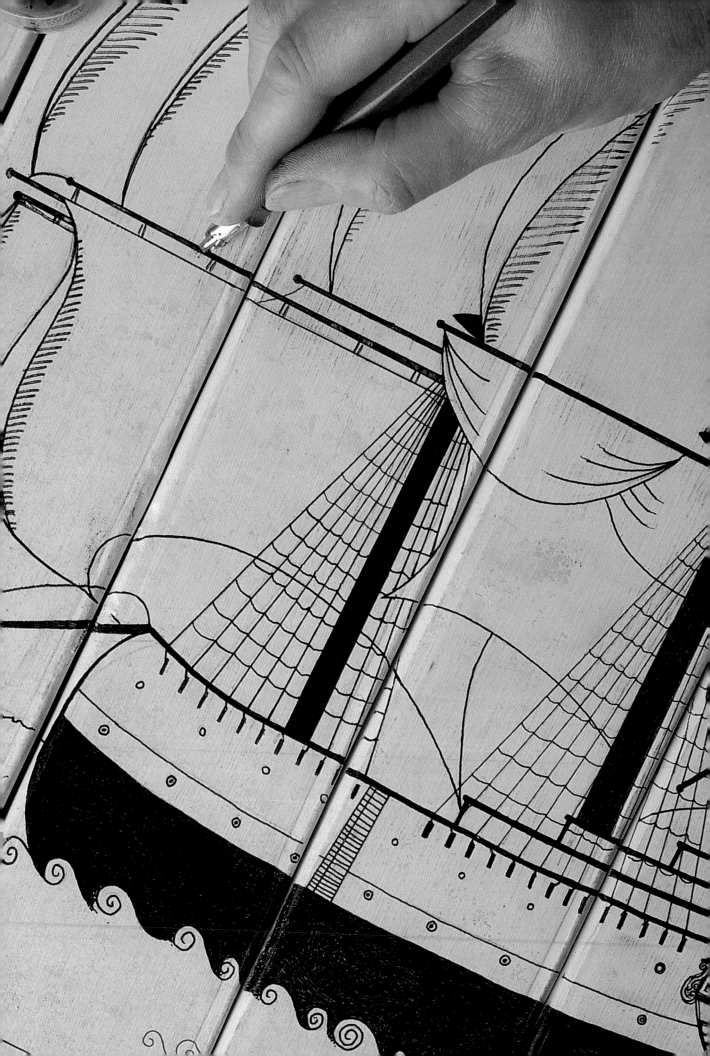

AN ELEGANT FILING SYSTEM

This filing cabinet is a clever little system, specially designed for those who like to keep their papers and documents neatly tucked away yet quick and easy to find. Although many of us now store household accounts and records in a home computer, there still remains the problem of filing documents such as mortgage and insurance contracts, tax papers, and so on. Reference material for hobbies, such as knitting and sewing patterns, cookery recipes, DIY information, and even love letters, need a home where they can easily be located.

Our inexpensive galleon storage system provides a stylish solution to the dilemma. Using the cheapest and strongest of materials, Medium Density Fibreboard (MDF), and sturdy box files, we created a slim piece of furniture which nevertheless has the capacity for storing a considerable amount of paperwork. And to add heirloom potential to this modern piece, we used an ancient Chinese design idea as inspiration.

The Chinese used storage chests consisting of a basic softwood frame placed on a low stand as far back as the Han Dynasty (206 BC-AD 25). Although the frames were plain and functional, the stands were often intricately carved, painted and gilded. Both case and stand were then lacquered, using layer upon layer of red or black slow-drying varnish, buffed to a high sheen.

MDF can be described as the twentieth-century equivalent of Chinese softwood – and with added advantages. It can be cut in any direction, as it has no grain, and it is flame and water retardant. Cheap to buy, it is heavy and durable enough to last at least a few lifetimes. It needs little or no preparation and its smooth, flat surface is the perfect base for a beautifully painted finish.

We layered our basic frame and stand with red and black water-based emulsion paint, which was lightly distressed, colour on colour, and varnished and polished to a soft sheen to give the appearance of expensive painted wood. The box files were simply painted in off-white emulsion and sponged in pale blue-grey. The galleon, clouds, sea and compass point were then traced onto the box-file spines and penworked in black ink to emulate all the charm of its ancient counterpart.

AN ELEGANT FILING SYSTEM
Techniques used:
Wood distressing, Sponging and Penwork

SHOPPING LIST

Frame and Stand (Distressing)

An MDF container and stand or equivalent
Fine-grade sandpaper
Fine-grade wire-wool
Half-litre wood primer
Half-litre tawny red emulsion
Half-litre black emulsion
$1\frac{1}{2}$-inch all-purpose decorating brush
Wax candle
Half-litre tin polyurethane clear satin varnish
Beeswax or furniture polish
Soft bristle brush

Box files (Sponging and Penwork)

12 standard box-files with plain spines
Workpaper Design B
12 Brass knobs
1-inch masking tape
Half-litre pale cream emuslsion
Quarter-litre blue/grey emulsion
Small sea sponge
$1\frac{1}{2}$-inch all-purpose decorating brush
Dressmaker's transfer paper
2B pencil
HB pencil
Eraser
Soft bristle brush
Black ink fine-liner pen
Clear satin polyurethane varnish

DISTRESSING THE FRAME AND STAND
Step-by-step

1.

MDF tends to cut with a hard edge. To improve the appearance of the painted finish, sand along any hard edges to soften and round them. Wipe over with a damp cloth and then paint a thin coat of wood primer over the entire piece. Allow to dry.

2.

Paint one smooth, dense coat of tawny red emulsion over the container and stand, covering all surfaces inside, outside and underneath, but *omitting the front edge of the middle shelf*. This will later be incorporated into the design on the box-file spines. When dry, repeat with a second coat of tawny red emulsion. Allow to dry.

3.

Firmly stroke the candle over the small areas of the frame and stand which would naturally wear with age – edges, up and down the sides and around the fretworked feet of the stand. Stroke and roll the candle sparingly in one direction (top to bottom) on the flat sides of the frame.

Painting tawny red emulsion onto the primed frame and stand.

Firmly stroking a candle over the sides of the frame.

DISTRESSING THE FRAME AND STAND
Step-by-step

4.

Paint the frame and stand smoothly with black emulsion, ensuring that all the tawny red colour is covered, but again omitting the front edge of the middle shelf. The inside of the frame and the under-neath of the stand should be left tawny red. Apply a second coat of black emulsion. Allow to dry thoroughly.

5.

Polish over the entire coat of black with fine-grade wire-wool, working in one direction until the tawny red base coat shows through the candle-waxed areas. Once more, omit the front edge of the middle shelf. Wipe over with a damp cloth.

Polishing the black emulsion with wire-wool to reveal red undercoat.

6.

Apply two to three coats of clear satin polyurethane var-nish over all painted areas. When dry, polish the piece with beeswax or furniture pol-ish, using a soft, lint-free cloth.

SPONGING AND PENWORK ON THE BOX FILES
Step-by-step

1.
Paint a smooth coat of pale cream emulsion over the front and back covers and spines of the box-files, and along the front edge of the middle shelf of the frame, masking off the surrounding areas with masking tape. Apply a second coat of cream paint to the files and allow to dry.

2.
Place the box files in the frame, and lay the piece of furniture flat with the spines upward.

3.
Pour a little blue/grey emulsion into a saucer, and use a damp sea sponge to dab the colour where the sea and sky areas will appear in the finished design. Soften any hard edges with the dampened sponge, blending the paint into the cream background.

4.
Reduce or enlarge Workpaper Design B on a photocopier to fit the area of the box file spines in the frame. Attach the workpaper to the spines using masking tape, and transfer the design in pencil onto the spines (*see* page 80), and across the front edge of the centre

Using a sea sponge to dab on blue/grey emulsion for the sea and sky.

Transferring the workpaper design onto the box-file spines.

shelf of the frame. Ensure that all the outlines are pencilled in and remove the Workpaper.

5.

Draw over the pencilled outlines of the design with a black fine-line pen. Use a ruler for straight lines and if necessary paint out any mistakes with a small watercolour brush and the pale cream background colour.

6.

Remove the box files from the frame and varnish front, back covers and spines with two smooth coats, and also include the edge of the middle shelf. The box-files can be sponged clean when necessary. Attach the brass knobs to the top of the spines of the top row of box-files and to the bottom of the spines of those on the lower row, avoiding the galleon penworked design itself.

Using a black fine-liner pen to draw over the pencilled design.

A KITCHEN CUPBOARD

The whole galleon design is here simply transferred and penworked onto a plain, cream-painted front panel of a wooden kitchen cupboard. The subdued colours and simple graphics of the piece are ideally suited to a country kitchen style.

A DECORATED BEDHEAD

On a warm summer's day I drove around the west of England in search of an old and dignified bedhead to restore and paint. Rumour had it that secondhand bedheads were everywhere to be found in the local villages, and I had in mind something large and magnificent with claw feet and clever carving that I could cover in gold leaf. I finally found the only bedhead that was, in fact, to be had that day – a modest reproduction hiding in the darkest corner of a junkyard, for which I had to negotiate a hard bargain. It was the worst possible example of mass-production, manufactured about forty years ago and probably discarded soon afterwards, the sort of piece of furniture that no-one else would dream of buying.

Once I had it out in the sunshine, the piece brightened up considerably, and a tentative area of decorative fretwork even appeared at the top of the frame. Usefully, it was already stripped, and it consisted of a large expanse of plain, flat panel on which to unleash my creative imagination. Opulent gold leaf was obviously not appropriate to such a modest piece; the approach had to be simple and fresh in deference to its more humble origins.

Using the fretwork pattern as a starting point, I devised a trailing leaf and flower design in translucent blue and white, such as might be found on a piece of antique porcelain. To authenticate this idea further, I decided to cover the surface of the bedhead with a network of fine cracks, such as you might find on an old blue-and-white vase.

This is called crackleglazing, a modern technique which emulates a process developed in eighteenth-century France in imitation of fashionable oriental furniture and pottery. The French *craquelure* consisted of a quick-drying (water-based) varnish painted over a slow-drying (oil-based) varnish. I used a much simpler method. Over a standard oil-based polyurethane clear varnish, I brushed on a thin coat of water-based gum arabic. This refined resin from the Acacia tree is now widely available. The simple combination produced random fine cracks over the bedhead which when rubbed with blue oil-colour took on the translucent freshness of an antique vase. Once a neglected eyesore, my bedhead now stands proudly in the sunshine from the bedroom window.

A DECORATED BEDHEAD
Techniques used:
Transfer painting and Crackleglazing

SHOPPING LIST

Wood or wood substitute bedhead
Medium-grade sandpaper
Quarter-litre white emulsion
Wet-and-dry sandpaper
Workpaper Design C
HB pencil
Quarter-litre Dutch blue emulsion
Prussian blue acrylic tube colour
No. 3 and No. 6 watercolour brushes
1½-inch flat decorating brush
200ml bottle gum arabic
Half-litre satin or matt clear polyurethane varnish
Household detergent
Tube of blue oil colour
Fine-bristle or varnish brush

PAINTING THE FLOWER AND LEAF DESIGN
Step-by-step

1.
Sandpaper the stripped bed-head back and front with medium-grade paper.

2
Paint a smooth coat of white emulsion on the back and front of the bedhead. When dry, sandpaper with wet-and-dry to produce a finish which is as porcelain-smooth as poss-ible. Paint on a second coat and sand again.

3.
Transfer the design outline only onto the front of the bed-head using Workpaper Design C (*see* page 80).

4.
Paint in the flowers, leaves and stems of the design using Dutch blue and a No. 6 brush. Two or three coats may be necessary for a good coverage.

5.
Fix on the Workpaper again with masking tape, taking care to replace it in exactly the right position. With the HB pencil and transfer paper, transfer the fine details of flowers and leaf veins onto the flat-painted areas. Remove the workpaper.

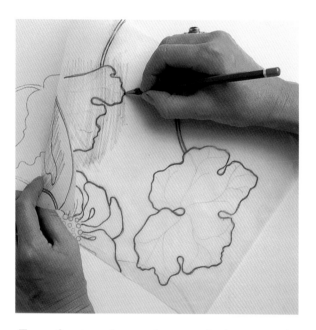

Transferring the workpaper design onto the bedhead, marking outlines only.

Painting in the flowers, stems and leaves in Dutch blue.

PAINTING THE FLOWER AND LEAF DESIGN
Step-by-step

6.

Squeeze about half an inch of the Prussian blue acrylic paint onto a saucer and mix to a creamy consistency with a little water. Paint on the detailed lines with a No. 3 brush, aiming for a lively, painterly effect rather than precision. Any mistakes can be erased with background colour.

7.

Erase any remaining pencil guidelines or smudges. Polyurethane varnish over the front and back of the bedhead to isolate and protect the painted design before applying the crackleglaze. Allow to dry.

Replacing the workpaper to transfer the details of the design.

Painting over the detail lines with Prussian blue acrylic.

CRACKLEGLAZING
Step-by-step

1.

With a fine bristle brush, paint a uniform and thin coat of polyurethane all over the bedhead. Wait about forty minutes for it to dry until it is slightly tacky, giving only the smallest pull to your finger. A dry 'tack' is better than an overly wet one.

2.

Pour the gum arabic into a shallow container and add a scant teaspoon of household detergent. This enables the water-based gum arabic to 'stretch' over the oil-based polyurethane. Paint a thin coat over the entire bedhead and allow to dry overnight. Fine cracks will begin to appear as the varnish and gum arabic dry out.

3.

Gently rub the blue oil paint over the bedhead with a soft, lint-free cloth, making sure that the colour catches in all the cracks which have appeared. Allow to set.

Painting on a thin coat of polyurethane varnish.

Rubbing blue oil paint into the cracks.

CRACKLEGLAZING
Step-by-step

4.

Remove any surplus colour and clean up the surface by wiping with a cloth dampened with white spirit. When all layers are completely dry, varnish with two coats of polyurethane.

Using a cloth with a little white spirit to wipe off excess paint colour.

BED AND BREAKFAST

The same flower and leaf motif has here been painted onto a white-painted breakfast tray, a simple idea which matches the bed-head beautifully.

A CLASSIC
DINING TABLE

There is something particularly friendly about a round dining table. The conversation flows easily and everyone can reach the food. A circular table is also a lot easier to arrange in a small dining room, as it tucks away into awkward corners, leaving plenty of floor space.

We made our classic dining table from scratch out of MDF (medium density fibreboard) and decorated the circular top with the subtlest of pale marble effects. We then applied dramatic *découpage* motifs of magpies and pearls, choosing tones which enhanced the colour scheme. The magpie motif was inspired by *Birds of Town and Village*, a book featuring beautiful reproductions of Basil Ede's bird paintings. However, any design – butterflies, flowers, shells, for example – can be photocopied from books or other sources and used in this way. The beauty of the piece depends on the almost monochromatic tones of the birds' wings and the sheen of pearls which reflects the tones of the opalescent painted marble background. The table looks so sophisticated that it is hard to believe that it has been made from such basic and inexpensive materials.

Découpage is a technique which was developed by Viennese craftsmen in the late seventeenth century to imitate the expensive, hand-painted furniture which was in great demand at the time. The word simply means 'cutting out', and their solution was to stick printed cut-outs onto inexpensive – in those days – *papier mâché* furniture, and then to sink them under many layers of varnish. This rendered the edges of the cut-outs invisible, and the decoration appeared to be painted by hand. These fakes cost very little to produce and could be sold at a healthy profit. They were so attractive that they soon became more collectable than the furniture they were imitating.

In Victorian England, *découpage* became very popular as a leisure time distraction for gentleladies, who decorated a plethora of household objects in this way – trays, boxes and screens were typical subjects. Their arrangements of cut-outs were often chaotic and their subject-matter sentimental. Since the 1950s, American craftspeople have become adept at the art, and they have expanded the technique to a system of layering several copies of the cut-outs to produce a 3D effect. *Découpage* is now an extremely versatile medium, as our second use of the magpie motifs on a very different background – an old painted tin chest – demonstrates.

A CLASSIC DINING TABLE
Techniques used:
Imitation marbling and Découpage

SHOPPING LIST

Wood or wood substitute dining table
Fine-grade sandpaper
Half-litre wood primer
Litre white vinyl silk emulsion paint
Litre acrylic scumble glaze
Fine wet-and-dry sandpaper
Grey acrylic tube colour
Raw umber acrylic tube colour
2 1½-inch flat decorating brushes
Sea sponge
Soft bristle or varnish brush
Half-litre clear matt polyurethane varnish
Photocopied *découpage* papers
Small bottle White Polish
Small sharp scissors or scalpel
Gum arabic
Half-litre polyurethane satin varnish
Methylated spirits for cleaning brushes

MARBLING THE TABLE
Step-by-step

1.

If your table is made of MDF, lightly sand the edges with medium-grade sandpaper to smooth and round off any hard edges. Wipe over with a damp cloth and apply one coat of wood primer. Sand lightly.

2.

Paint the tabletop and base smoothly with white vinyl silk emulsion. Marbling needs a very flat base, so apply two or three coats, sanding in between with wet-and-dry paper.

Applying acrylic scumble glaze over the painted tabletop.

3.

Apply a thin coat of acrylic scumble glaze over the tabletop and base. This transparent glaze helps the marble colours glide on easily and remain wet and workable for a longer time.

4.

Squeeze ½-inch of raw umber acrylic colour onto a plate containing scumble glaze, and mix. Using a damp sea sponge, draw thin 'vein' lines diagonally and at random across the surface. Repeat the same process using the grey acrylic colour.

Sponging on the first marble veins with a damp sea sponge.

MARBLING THE TABLE
Step-by-step

5.

With a clean, dry decorating brush, stipple over the painted veins with a bouncing action, holding the brush vertically and spreading the paint from the centre of the veins outwards, fading them into the white background.

6.

Using a soft bristle brush, lightly whisk the tips of the bristles across the veins, further softening and blending them. Allow to dry and varnish the table with matt polyurethane varnish.

Whisking the tips of the brush over the veins to blend and soften them.

APPLYING THE *DÉCOUPAGE* MOTIFS
Step-by-step

1.
Photocopy your chosen design motifs, if necessary enlarging or reducing them. Paint over the entire photocopies with white polish to stiffen the paper. They will be easier to cut out, providing sharper edges to the motifs.

2.
When dry, cut out using the scissors or scalpel. Manoeuvre the paper rather than the scissors. Cut into tight corners from the outside of the motif inwards to produce a sharp finish.

3.
Arrange the cut-outs on the tabletop to produce the best design. Mark their positions lightly with a pencil.

4.
Paste the backs of the motifs with gum arabic and stick them in their marked positions. Paint gum arabic over the top, extending over the edges of the cut-outs to secure them firmly. Wipe over with a lint-free cloth to remove excess gum.

5.
When dry, paint over each of the cut-outs with white polish to 'fix' them. Then apply two coats of satin polyurethane varnish over the entire piece.

Cutting out the magpie motif with sharp scissors.

Painting over the magpie cut-out with gum arabic.

A MAGPIE'S TREASURE CHEST

The *découpage* design of magpies, together with cut-outs of oak leaves and acorns, adapts surprisingly well to an old metal chest. The chest itself has been stippled with blue and green paint over an olive green base before the application of the motifs.

AN INLAID CUPBOARD

We bought this sensible cupboard for very little money in a secondhand shop. Unadorned and functional, it had plenty of deep, useful shelves and we chose it because the wood was in good condition and unvarnished – saving us the strenuous trouble of stripping it. Unlike some, this inexpensive pine was a rich, golden colour which we used to full advantage as a background for our decoration.

We devised an imitation of marquetry – inlaid wood veneer – using an acorn and leaf design which we made into a stencil. Some of the most exciting and expensive items of earlier wooden furniture to be seen in museums and antique shops are those which use marquetry, a time-consuming and extremely skilled craft applied to oak furniture in Britain in Elizabethan times. Small pieces of coloured woods such as yew or holly were cut into the oak to produce contrasting patterns. Marquetry itself was developed in the seventeenth century using small slivers of light wood veneers – usually sycamore, apple or pear wood – combined with more exotic materials such as mother-of-pearl, brass and pewter. The pieces were glued onto panels to be inserted into softwood furniture carcasses. Marquetry craftsmen produced wonderful geometric designs, and bold flower patterns, for which they ingeniously tinted the wood by dipping the veneers into hot sand. Later they developed even more intricate designs, called 'seaweed', which were characteristically used on items such as clockcases and mirror frames.

Our imitation uses a stencil and wood stain, a simplified, twentieth-century version of the technique which is very effective. The authenticity of the finished piece relies on the basic colour of the piece of furniture. If it is already attractive, you need only sandpaper it and wipe it over with a 70/30 solution of vinegar and water to neutralize any oil or grease on the surface of the wood. If the piece is made of new wood, you may like to stain it first with woodstain. This is an effect which works wonderfully well as a border or all-over design on stripped floorboards, and can also be adapted to smaller wooden pieces such as picture frames.

AN INLAID CUPBOARD
Techniques used:
Reverse stencilling and Woodstaining

SHOPPING LIST

Piece of stripped wood furniture
Workpaper Design D
Dressmaker's transfer paper
2B pencil
No. 6 watercolour brush
Half-litre woodstain in light oak colour
Quarter-litre woodstain in medium oak colour
Litre brightly coloured vinyl matt emulsion paint (for inside of cupboard)
1½-inch decorating brush
Half-litre satin polyurethane varnish
Black ink fine-liner pen
75 ml masking fluid
Beeswax or furniture polish
Scalpel
Fine wire-wool

REVERSE STENCILLING WITH WOODSTAIN
Step-by-step

1.

Transfer Workpaper Design D to your chosen piece (*see* page 80). Give some thought to the arrangement of the motifs: use the main body of the design to cover large areas and smaller sections of acorns and leaves to fill in corners. If necessary, adapt the size of the motifs on a photocopier.

2.

Paint in the motifs using a No. 6 watercolour brush and masking fluid. If the fluid 'bleeds' beyond the outlines, stop and score round them with a scalpel. The fluid paints on milky white, but dries transparent.

3.

When dry, paint over the entire piece of furniture with light oak woodstain, working it in until you have the density of colour you want.

4.

While the stain is drying, paint the inside of the piece of furniture in a bright colour –we chose a tawny red vinyl matt emulsion. Allow to dry.

Transferring the workpaper design onto the cupboard.

Painting over the acorns, stems and leaves with masking fluid.

REVERSE STENCILLING WITH WOODSTAIN
Step-by-step

5.

Gently rub away the masking fluid with a finger or the tip of a scalpel. This will reveal the leaves, acorns and stems in a paler wood colour.

6.

Using the No. 6 watercolour brush, darken the acorn shapes with medium oak woodstain.

Painting over the entire cupboard with light oak woodstain.

Gently lifting off the masking fluid with a scalpel.

7.

For an authentic marquetry inlay effect, draw round the outline of the acorns and oak-leaves with a black ink fine-liner pen.

8.

Paint the piece with polyurethane satin varnish with the decorating brush, and when dry gently rub over the piece with the wire-wool. Polish to a soft sheen with good furniture polish or beeswax.

Painting acorns with medium oak wood-stain.

Outlining the acorns and leaves with fine-liner pen.

AN OAKLEAF MIRROR FRAME

We used the same stencil motifs to decorate a simple, painted mirror frame, arranging sections of the designs to make up a linked design, white paint on maroon.

A DESIGNER DESK

The desk we used for this project is typical of many of the mass-produced pieces of furniture manufactured between the two World Wars, when thousands of identical items were churned out to supply a developing market for new furniture. Such pieces can now be found in secondhand shops, passed over in favour of contemporary flat-pack, self-assembly units, and can therefore be bought very cheaply. This furniture of a few decades in age is invariably coated with a treacly-brown stain, which now looks very unfashionable. Inter-War furniture is nevertheless usually well made from heavy woods such as mahogany or oak, with proper dove-tailed joints, and is worth resurrecting.

Our desk was made of heavy oak, and was completely unremarkable in design. It needed an inventive idea to lend it some originality. With great difficulty, we removed its plain wooden handles. The ensuing argument over the quickest and least stressful way of removing thick, brown varnish left us both somewhat weakened. Short of time and breath, we took the line of least resistance and sent it to be professionally stripped – not the cheapest option, but entirely effective. The desk was returned unveiled and vulnerably bare - ready for work. For those with the time and muscle commitment, details for the removal of ancient stains and varnishes are on page 77. After intensive stripping, the piece will need to be sanded down to remove any rough patches.

Oak has a pronounced and fairly coarse grain, so we decided to feature, rather than fight, its patterns by emphasising them with liming wax. Liming is a good technique to use on hardwoods with strong grain as it lightens them with a subtle, bleached appearance, like driftwood. The process is often used to stunning effect on floors and panelling as well as large items of furniture.

To make our desk unique, we then designed a chequered top of small, imitation marble squares. Years ago, apprentice cabinetmakers produced furniture which displayed various painting techniques in order to prove that they had learnt their trade. They were called apprentice pieces, and our desk is one such.

65

A DESIGNER DESK
Techniques used:
Wood liming and Marbling

MATERIALS

Oak desk liming
Medium-grade sandpaper
Half-litre tin liming wax
1½-inch decorating brush
Old, short-bristled brush
Half-litre green/blue emulsion paint
Large wire brush
Rubber gloves
Face mask
Soft lint-free cloths

Marble panels

Piece of card equivalent in size to marbled area
Wet-and-dry sandpaper
Quarter-litre cream emulsion paint
1½-inch all-purpose decorating brush
Pencil, ruler, eraser
Litre acrylic scumble glaze
Spray mount
Acrylic tube colours in olive green, raw umber, yellow ochre,
burnt sienna, iridescent white, black
Soft-bristle brush
No. 2 and No. 6 watercolour brushes
Flat wash watercolour brush
Litre clear satin or matt polyurethane varnish
1-inch masking tape

LIMING THE OAK
Step-by-step

1.

First firmly stick a piece of blank card with spray mount to the area of the desk to be marbled, in order to protect it from the liming.

2.

Soak all the surfaces of the desk to be limed to soften the grain. Do this outside, or lay down protective plastic and newspapers inside.

3.

Wire brush the wood in sections, working with the grain to remove any soft wood or dust and open up the grain. When thoroughly dry, smooth over the desk with fine-grade sandpaper and wipe with a soft cloth.

4.

Paint on green/blue emulsion diluted with 30% water with the decorating brush, working with the grain. The colour will lighten considerably with the liming wax, so a good depth should be applied. Allow to dry.

5.

Using a short-bristle brush and cloth, apply the liming wax, working it well into the grain with a circular, rubbing

Masking off the desk top area securely with card.

Using a wire brush to remove any soft wood or dust from the grain.

LIMING THE OAK
Step-by-step

movement. As long as the grain is completely filled with wax, it does not matter if the effect is patchy at this point. Work on a small area at a time.

6.

Leave the wax for ten minutes to harden, then polish in circular movements with a soft cloth. Press the wax down into the grain as you work and polish off any surplus. Leave to harden for ten minutes and then buff over with a clean, soft cloth.

Painting along the grain with blue/green emulsion.

Using a soft cloth to work the liming wax into the grain of the wood

Polishing with a soft cloth to remove excess wax.

MARBLING THE DESK TOP
Step-by-step

1.

Remove the protective card and mask the panel with 1-inch masking tape to give a clean, protective edge when painting. Paint on a thin coat of wood primer, and when dry two coats of cream emulsion, sanding in between for a smooth surface.

2.

Draw on the squares with a soft pencil, using a ruler. We have twenty-eight squares, but the number can be reduced to give larger, more manageable squares.

3

Mix raw umber and black acrylic colours with water in separate saucers to a creamy consistency, and paint a row of alternate, chequerboard squares across the area. Use a ruler or edge of the protective card to keep within the squares. The next row of cream squares is already in place as a background for the marbling. Fill the entire area in this way and allow to dry.

4.

Put a little olive green, raw umber, yellow ochre, burnt sienna, iridescent white and black acrylics separately in

Applying cream emulsion to the area to be marbled.

Painting in the squares using card to help keep the edges straight.

70

squeezes on a saucer. Pour a quarter-lite of scumble glaze onto a separate plate. Working on two or three squares at a time, brush a thin slip-coat of scumble onto the squares (to keep the flow of paint wet and smooth), then paint random, wavy lines with random colours diagonally across the squares with the No. 6 watercolour brush. Shake your hand slightly to imitate the vein of real marble. Our desk was worked in components of four squares, each coloured and veined differently, as follows:

Cream base emulsion with olive green and raw umber veins

Cream base emulsion with yellow ochre and burnt sienna veins

Black acrylic base with iridescent white veins

Raw umber acrylic base with burnt sienna veins

Softening the veins with a dry brush.

5.

Soften the lines by whisking the soft dry brush over the surface, blending them into the background.

6.

When you have completed all the squares, allow to dry and varnish with polyurethane.

7.

Working from left to right along the length of the diagonal squares, stick down masking tape strips approximately an eighth of an inch apart.

8.

Dilute black acrylic colour with a little water and using a No. 2 watercolour brush, paint between the strips of tape. When dry, remove the tape and apply new strips to paint lines from right to left, across the existing lines. Repeat around the edge of the panel. When dry, varnish with two coats of polyurethane.

Lining the edges of the squares with black paint between strips of masking tape.

AN OCCASIONAL TABLE

The same colours of chequerboard marbling are used here on a small occasional table, and have been framed by a grey painted, marbled border.

BASIC FURNITURE PREPARATION AND FINISHING TECHNIQUES

Although most of the pieces of furniture we have decorated for this book were chosen for their cheapness, blandness and ugliness – just to prove what can be achieved with paint – we did try to find some which did not need too much preparatory work. This is certainly worth bearing in mind, especially as there is so much secondhand furniture on the market that you can be selective about its quality. However, if you do have a piece in poor condition, the following techniques will help you prepare it for the more pleasurable activity of its decoration.

Unless you are liming, painting or stencilling onto bare wood, there is no need to strip off all old paint. When sanded smooth it provides a good base coat for new paint. It is essential to make sure that your chosen piece is free from woodworm and that all unnecessary screws and nails are removed from it. Otherwise, used furniture has seen something of life, and its dents and bruises are part of its character. Your aim should not be for a pristine finish, but for a mellow charm.

The quality of the paints which you will apply to decorate the furniture has never been better. Using modern technology, paint manufacturers are producing products which cling tenaciously, flow smoothly and dry to a very tough finish. Even the new water-based products are resilient as well as environmentally friendly.

THE PREPARATION OF OLD WOOD

WOOD IN REASONABLE CONDITION

Check all furniture, even that in reasonable condition, for wood-worm. These invisible little beetles not only destroy the piece of furniture over time, but will also migrate to other pieces. Each woodworm hole should be systematically treated with a de-worming product, preferably in winter when the beetles are dormant. A new woodworm polish is now available which will ensure that furniture stays free of woodworm after initial treatment.

Before starting decorative work on a piece, wipe it over with a 70/30 solution of vinegar and water to neutralize any remaining grease on the wood. Allow to dry and sand all over with medium-grade sandpaper. Take care to remove any flaking old paint. Dust or paint in awkward corners can be carefully removed with a pointed object – a screwdriver or nailfile. Wash with a mild solution of household detergent, rinse and allow to dry.

If there are deep or unsightly scars, paint into them with a small amount of undercoat or wood primer, then fill the crack with wood-filler so that it stands proud. Smooth level with a damp cloth after about ten minutes and then allow the filler to dry out completely. Sandpaper smooth.

If the decoration you are intending requires a very smooth surface, you might consider giving the furniture two good coats of acrylic gesso, sanding in between. Acrylic primer is a cheaper alternative. Acrylic gesso can also be added to water-based paints to make them tougher.

WOOD IN POOR CONDITION

Wobbly legs, loose handles and the like should all be firmly fixed back into place. If the piece is covered in many layers of chipped paint or old varnish, it will be quicker and more effective in the long run to strip it off completely. Paint stripper must be used outside or with windows open, and it is essential to wear gloves and a protective face-mask. Leave the stripper to work into the paint and then wash off thoroughly or hose down. When totally dry, smooth with medium-grade sandpaper. A final sanding, to give a smooth finish, should be done with wet-and-dry paper, and steel- or wire-wool can be used around curves and mouldings. When sanding, the strokes should follow the grain of the wood.

Stripped wood should always be primed with one smooth coat of wood primer before painting.

NEW OR UNFINISHED WOOD

If you have decided to add some character to self-assembly or new, mass-produced furniture, check first that it is not coated with pro-tective wax. This should be removed by wiping over with white spirit and then sanding as for older furniture. Keep any water away from the piece, as new wood absorbs it very readily.

New wood has a greater occurrence of knots, which need to be sealed before painting, as new paint will react with the resin in the wood and 'bleed' brown stains through. A shellac sealing preparation called 'knotting' is now available, which should be painted in two or three coats. Employ normal sanding when the piece is dry.

MDF (MEDIUM DENSITY FIBREBOARD)

This will need little or no preparation. Any sharp edges can be sanded with medium- or fine-grade sandpaper and a coat of wood primer will give a smooth surface on which to paint.

METAL AND TIN

Metal garden furniture, tin trays, boxes or metal light fittings should all be primed with metal primer before painting to prevent any future rust. Remove any flaking paint or rust with medium-grade sandpaper, wipe over with white spirit and then apply the primer.

PLASTIC OR TILES

The tough, dense surfaces of such materials must be broken to provide a 'key' for the paint to flow into and cling to. Coarse wire-wool will break the surface imperceptibly. Tile primer is also now available to provide a good, absorbent base for paint. Use oil-based paints, ceramic or gloss paints for a long-lasting finish.

FINISHING VARNISHES

POLYURETHANE

All painted furniture must be varnished to safeguard the precious artwork underneath from daily wear and tear. Best known of all varnishes now are the general purpose polyurethanes, which are oil-based and suitable for most painted effects. They are made with matt (no shine), satin (semi-shine) and gloss (high shine) finishes. It is preferable to specify Clear Varnish, as some polyurethanes have a yellowish tone which spoils the clarity of the paler shades of paint underneath.

Matt varnish is best suited to painting on rougher surfaces: wood with a pronounced grain, for example. Satin is the most widely used as it gives a pleasing sheen to many finished pieces. Gloss is the toughest finish, which should be used for kitchen, bathroom or garden furniture. The solvent for poyurethane varnishes is white spirit.

ACRYLIC

These are comparatively new on the market, and are available in the same three finishes as polyurethane. They have a quicker drying time as they are water-solvent, and are best used over furniture decorated with water-based paints. Acrylic varnishes do not yellow with age, and are becoming popular as a more environmentally sound alternative.

VARNISHING BRUSHES

Any soft-bristled decorating brush is suitable. A chisel-headed brush, with graduated bristles cut straight across the tip will deliver the varnish a little at a time, producing a smooth, even layer.

Dip the brush into the varnish so that it is loaded halfway up the bristles, wiping off any excess on the rim of the tin. Place the brush in the centre of the area to be varnished, and brush out smoothly towards the sides. Work in one direction with the first coat, and across in the other for the second to avoid obvious brush marks.

USING THE WORKPAPERS

Here are two methods of transferring the designs on the Detachable Workpapers to the piece of furniture itself.

Using transfer paper

1.

If the workpaper design is not the correct size to fit your chosen piece, use a photocopier to enlarge or reduce it.

2.

Trim the photocopy to fit the area you are working on. Where practicable, it is best to arrange the main body of the designs onto the larger areas to be decorated and the smaller components around them.

3.

Place dressmaker's transfer paper (or handwriting carbon paper) face down onto the area to be worked, and place the workpaper or photocopy face up on top. Attach both firmly to the piece with low-tack masking tape.

4.

Draw over the design with a hard (HB) pencil, taking care not to press so hard that you will score the wood. Work systematically from left to right and top to bottom of the design, occasionally lifting a corner of the workpaper to check that all the lines have been transferred.

5.

Remove transfer and workpapers. Clean off any mistakes or smudges with a soft pencil eraser.

Using pencil

1.

If necessary, enlarge or reduce the workpaper as above.

2.

Scribble on the back of the workpaper or photocopy with a soft (2B) pencil, covering every part of the design.

3.

Place the workpaper scribble side down onto the piece of furniture and attach firmly with masking tape.

4.

Draw over the design with a hard (HB) pencil, as above.